When it Matters

When it Matters

Don Ennis

Xulon Press Elite

Xulon Press Elite
2301 Lucien Way #415
Maitland, FL 32751
407.339.4217
www.xulonpress.com

Printed in the United States of America.

Paperback ISBN-13: 978-1-6628-1155-5
Ebook ISBN-13: 978-1-6628-1156-2

Tim puts out his press release on the frontline of life and human rights. He knows God wants a better way. Jesus is a means of protection for me, and you will see what happens when we come together. For me, God's way has been great for growth in our hearts due to this man's view on he lives his life. I not only believe his word, but also his ability to see his beauty. I see his face in heaven for a few minutes before they speak. It is done with God today and always. Seeing Him in a time of need is my truth in this life, and I fear for His return from His glory. Real change within me occurs in God's best time, and my faith in mankind, my faith is driven by God's grace, with all His glory.

I ran through the meadows. The tall flowers touched my fingers. They swayed in the wind. I ran through the meadows with a confidence in you, my Father in heaven, for a new life mission is a means of freedom. I ran through the meadows with the truth of our humanity in which God has been missing from us. I ran through the meadows of His grace in His name. I ran through the meadows of the house of God with all His glory.

Tim has been a member of Congress for several years now. He said in a statement from his office that he will not waver from his perspective on this issue because he knows Christ's great way for growth in the world. Tom wants to hear from you about the future with your life and how he can handle the situation. Tom and Tim have been a secret for the past three years. They know what the enemy will say. They work for the people, by the people. They know that God created all of us equally in His image. They love God even more then their careers. Here on earth, they love each other just as much. They will never forget that God will restore all of us equally in this world. God is the best way to get rid of the infection in our hearts due to this disease we face in the world.

Tim has been a bit different from this moment of silence. He seems to be in a bad place and cannot turn off the world. Tim knows Mark loves him, but Tim feels so alone in this world. Only Jesus knows what He is doing in the world. He calls out to God daily and knows what he must do. Tim calls out the dance of his life. He looks to please God. Many times, Tim struggles to believe God won't fail him. He takes the time to stop being so angry about the future because he did it to himself. Only when Tim is honest with himself can the road of life become smoother than what it is now. He will not give up the sky for a moment. His prayers for his forgiveness is of essence and time, and his faith will continue until his death, and his own skin will become more of a good result, all in the name of Christ.

Due to the past mistakes Tim has made that make him vulnerable to the world and humanity, the enemy has been at the door to make sure Tim would go through a difficult relationship. The enemy has a way of doing life so that the ability to talk to Christ is avoided. Tim knows where he sees fit to fill his life with God today. The energy Tim gives to chasing temptation is not equivalent to the love that Jesus will give him. It only proves to be a temporary fix, and lately, not even that.

Shelia comes home. She takes her heels off and plops on the sofa. Her job is getting to her, and has caused her stress. It drains the life out of her daily.

She knows you have plans for her life and she is doing the right thing by you. Lord, give her the opportunity to make a decision to make it happen right now and see how things coming along with her husband and how they feel about the future of life. Shelia lives for Jesus, and in this time of need, you have the right direction of your life so that it can fill out the fire. Rise for a new normal life to live for Jesus.

Shelia just not sure why you think of the world to heal the loneliness of her dreams yet again. They have to choose from our perspective in this world in which God has a hold on her life.

Shelia needs to feel love, not just the spiritual. She needs to feel her husband in her isolation. They need to get back to be one unit. They need to feel each other's skin, and the rhythm of the dance, the moments of pleasure. They had a usually day at work and passion turns into something real with her husband that he will restore all the other times over the devil.

The heart that beats for Jesus is a heart that is alive.
The heart that beats for Jesus knows no more games or anything else that is not perfect.
The heart of Jesus is wide open to you today.
The heart is where you find yourself in the house of God.

The heart that burns for Jesus also beats for Jesus.
The heart is where you find yourself in the house of God.
The house of God is where your heart beats for three.
The house of God is the best way to get to know you better and be active in your life.

Day one

The scene set
Jack needs to get across town,
So he puts ad in paper.
Lexie needs the money,
So she answers the ad.
They talk on the phone.
They agree to meet the next day at Dunkin.
They will drive for a few days.
Will this work?
Will they discover more about life?
They are two strangers in a moment of need.
They are going by trust that they have to choose between
fear and hope.
As night falls, they both wonder.
They were talking with you, Jesus.
You answered the need and the solution.
You will guide them and keep them safe.
They both close their eyes.
They will need the rest.
This trip will take some twist and turns.
No matter what, Christ is a means of protection as the road
trip goes ahead.

Day two

The morning of the meet,
Lexie gets there first.
As she waits, she watches people in and out of Dunkin.
She sees singles
She sees couples
She sees guy couples
She sees female couples
After all, she is in America.
Suddenly, a man approaches.
He looks average,
But sexy.
He says, "Hello, I am Jack."
"Hi, I am Lexie."
Thank yous enter the air.
They shake hands
"So, are we ready to go, Jack?"
"Yes, Lexie."
They proceed to get into her Lexus.
Doors shut,
And car starts.
They pull away onto the road.
Where it leads is a mystery that Jesus can answer.

The heart that beats for Jesus is one that will be content in his own skin. The image of her dreams and hard work in essential detail for your sake protect her from harm. Christ gives her a sense of value in the world and humanity from His life in a simplistic mind to say that she steps into her new song from the house of God…

Christ, I look in the mirror; the image is blurred and I am very upset by this. I can see two images, the one God loves and the one that the world sees everyday. The world is far from what God sees; it affects my heart, and my soul weighs heavy on my mind. It's so tiring sometimes.

Christ lives in me. He is this force that says one more day. I have much in store for you; you are not to listen to the enemy. My destiny and the plan have beauty all over it till the end of time. You are the vision I created. See the light and hear the beauty. I will restore the balance of perspective on God's change in you now.

The reason I exist here is that I am a child of God with all His glory. We all are the hope for our humanity. We can change the direction of our humanity in this time of need. Christ will be the best way you deliver your love for the world. The world is very divided and we need to talk about everything, big and small, so we can do this right. The world is full of joy and promise. We can be open-minded to make a great place for the people of America. The Jesus we all hear about is ready to take a look at the end result of trusting Jesus by making a decision to take the responsibility of our depression and the truth of our lives. When we do this, not only will we be in a better place, we can also heal the wounds that have started to build up. The promise of tomorrow is now. In Jesus' name, I confess this is the most precious of all time, just like the angels of mercy God sent, singing their new song from the house of God.

Today was slow.
A large scale of distracted mind drove it.
All it could do was have a good reason why I am so excited for this revival of my life.
I am here, and I walk with God today and always by His grace. The scope of Jesus in every moment of silence is nothing personal, and it is worth noting that there are some images for a new life mission that will change your mind for yourself, and others will be amazed by how much you love Him without any explanation.
Christ, bestow your soul in the world and humanity, for its beauty will come back into our society and our children's lives will be better for it.

Today I worry,
Then have to remember,
You are in control, and You are the way.
You will keep me safe from the enemy.
Everything proceeding with You will work out.
I know this isn't over till You say it is.
You are my savior now, and may I always have the strength of Your hands.
You are the only person who has the power to make sure it gets better with time and energy in the house of God.

Jesus, walk with me, and my life forever has been a little more of Your life and Your love for me. I never want anything or anyone else more than I want You. You are my savior, and

I will never forget that You have a mission in my heart to be a force of life in the world.

I have to stop the carnage of our humanity, and the world is in danger of losing our hearts due to this disease we face.

God, all I do is for You always.
Jesus is the best way to live for Him.
Christ, bestow the journey of the human spirit.
Let the angel sing new songs from the hills of new release in the spiritual life.
In Jesus, I walk proudly.
In God, I live in the moment of truth.
In Christ, I long for a MINISTRY.
Angel of mercy, shower me with love and joy.

You are to dig deep with your FEET.
You cannot give into the doubt that holds you back.
Set your mind on Christ in the heavens.
He will give you a sense of value in your life.
He will not fail you.
The moment the enemy is working hard to prove it wasn't a good life; you have to be ready, with Jesus and His grace.
God loves the way you live your life, and He will not let the enemy bring you down.
Do what you set your mind to do.
Then pray to God and let Him hear you.
Shout out loud to Jesus.
Say, "I am not afraid of the enemy. In Jesus' name, I will overcome.
You are not perfect, but you are the result of trusting Jesus and His character.

Where you find yourself in the world is full of happiness and joy in the house of God.

The heart wants what it wants.
The difference is knowing if it's coming from God.
The reason you must know what they say about Him is because He has the comfort of being able to bring the best quality to your life.
The reason why God doesn't make me feel bad is because he comforts my feelings and the dreams of my life forever in the house of God.
The heart holds all the secrets of the world and humanity, for the house of God is the only way we can do it together.
With your help, we will not be done with God, and He is your best friend.

Today, just for moment, the enemy tried to get hold of my worry.
Then I reminded the enemy how much Jesus loves me.
I was not having an effect from the enemy.
The omega and I are a team.
He restores.
I believe in God, and He loves me anyway.

Today, I am weary.
I am not confident.
But I know God worked His love for me.
He made a way.
He gives me a sign.
He showed me the way.
He was ready to go out into the light of my strength
To brighten my darkness,
To take my vision to my life,

To raise the minimum for a new way,
To be honest with the truth of this vision of my life.
So pray to God and love the moment He will restore all that
He will restore in my heart.
When in doubt, don't give into your thoughts.
Instead, use them to reach out to the house of God.
Go to Christ and pray for God to heal your soul.
He gives me peace in the storm.
When the rain falls, I'm dry.
When the odds roll in the enemy's favor, God just raises my
mind to say no more to the world and humanity, for the
enemy's fears are not going anywhere in this heart of mine.

The heart that burns for God
The heart that burns for Jesus
The heart that burns for Christ

I have been given a chance to help others through my own
experience in life. I am ready to serve Jesus and pray for the
world to heal the loneliness of your life and for your family
to have the right direction of His plan.

We will never forget that you continue your work with the
house of God, with love for His greatness; for your sake, with
Christ's help, protect your child from the enemy.

Burn. My heart burns for Jesus, the omega of all. It's on fire
for the Christ who died for you and me.

The hearts burns for the world and humanity in which God
has been missing since the beginning of time. I will never
have patience with the world's excuses if God is not in my
life, but my life forever has been changed for the better.

Burn for Jesus.
Burn for God.
Burn for Christ.
Burn for Christ and pray for peace.
Burn for Jesus and His angels.

Burning heart, beat upon Jesus today. Let His love come to you, free of any kind of judgment as you reveal your heart to others through God. Burning soul, keep the flames of red light; burn with color in your eyes, open for you always; refuse to believe that you are not good enough.

Today was a slow day. It just dragged on and on. But the whole time, I thought about you, God; how You gave me my name, and my future lines up for the house of God, living all the way for Jesus. You have put me on a new road, and I will get through this time of fear. You are using me as your witness, and your love for me will shine on our hearts from the beginning of time.

I will not sway from You.
I will not leave the church.
I will not let the enemy and his fears set forth in my mind.
I will never agree with the world of darkness.
I will not be defined by my own limits.
I will not be defined in any way other than by my Christ.
I willingly thought that I was going forward, knowing you were saying goodbye, but I could not do anything for him. I miss my dad.
I am very proud of your life, so I stay away from the enemy and the fears of our humanity.
Christ will restore.
Jesus will save my soul.
God will revive my soul.

Christ, I am tired today. I am on overload. You are the way to my salvation. I look in the mirror and don't like what I see or have become. I am in a state of limbo and am becoming more of who You want me to be. You give me light to help me keep going toward Him, yet the fears are deep, and forever I can be open-minded to the house of God. Have faith in what is your approach to this point, I think. God knows I am strong enough to calm waters, and I am very grateful for this revival of my strength. God will not let the storm get away with the chains that are so tightly bound to me and held by the enemy.

God, release the chains that bind me.
Jesus, break the chains that hold me.
Christ, strip me of the world's chains the enemy has placed on me.

Pray to God.
Pray to Jesus.
Pray to Christ.
Pray for the world and humanity, for its sake, to change our lives and our children's lives.

Lord, I ache today. I get in over my head trying to be all that I can be. I spread myself far and wide. Oh, Lord, help me slow down. Help me up anytime You see me falling. Help me stop the insanity of fast-tracking in my life. Let me know and see what Christ has in store for me.

I pray to God.
I pray to Jesus.
I pray to Christ.
I have faith in You, creator of my essence.
Just want to write my books.

Just want to see Your face in this world.
Just want to be with You.

I look to the higher heavens as an independent person who
has been missing since the beginning of my life.

I look to God for a new normal; they are to be in Jesus' name,
and His character is the best way to look forward and clear
your head of expectations that are not real or placed by
God's design.
God lets you speak.
Humans want to be in charge.
God has plan for your life.
Others want to be your boss.
I give my heart to God.
I live for Jesus.
I look to Christ.

You can't change history.
You can learn from it.
You can teach your children new ways and God's way.
You are responsive and in charge of your role in the world.
Never lose hope.
Have hope always.
Never forget to pray.
Pray daily.
Never forget to love.
Live, and love God.
Love Jesus.
Love Christ.
Never lose faith.
Have faith in all you do.

We are the future.
Pray to God.
We are the answer to every challenge.
Pray to Jesus.
We are the solution to every problem.
Pray to Christ.
We are the connection to unity.
Have faith in your God.
Have faith Christ will give you the right direction of His plan,
and His character is the best way to get rid of the infection
that CAUSES you pain and loss of heart.

We are the change.
Pray to God.
We have the passion for them.
Pray to Jesus.
We need the energy of the house of God.
Pray to Christ.
We are a great team.
Have faith in Christ.
We are in need of calm heads.
Go to God.
Have faith Christ will give you the power to be a force of God
Pray to God.
Have faith in mankind to understand what happened, and
what takes place in the house of God.
Have a mission to forge ahead in my life and human
connections.

Beauty lived in all of us.
It's here and now.
It's a challenge to see how things are happening.
It's the best way to live for Jesus.

It's the same as what Christ says about it before you enter the house of God.

It's a great way to get to know the better part of your family.

It's the only way to live for Jesus and his COMMANDS.

It's the only thing that keeps me from getting into a messy situation.

Beauty lives in all of us.

Beauty is there any way you are. You are God's creation, and He will restore all that you need. You are not meant to be like everyone else. You are not to compare nor be compared to anyone else.

Beauty is a means of blinders for mankind. We tend to judge the person from the outside rather than the heart. We look at the surface and see what we want to see. This saddens God because He has the right creation, and left His soul in the body of His children.

Beauty is a design and a sense of value to God's heart, and He loves our imperfect selves, for our value is not just on the outside; He knows that this is all temporary, yet true beauty is in the depth of His temple.

The beauty of His plan comes to us all.

Beauty is the best thing ever for the world to see the light of Jesus in every corner of the human spirit.

The beauty of this story is that we face a greater danger when we don't follow God, yet the beauty is that He loves us no matter what.

The scope of Jesus is wide enough for me to keep going forward with this new road.

The reason for this is that we face the challenge of having the opportunity to make a great place for the people of America. The strength they desire is in the house of God, with all your will to be a force from God to heal the loneliness that we face daily.

The revival is now in place until the world is full of happiness in our hearts; due to this, we must come together and create a new normal.

My mission:
You are in control of my life, and your love for me is my best source to answer the question of whether or not I am very proud of your life, so I stay away from the enemy and his fears. I really like this friendship going far and beyond here and now. So many times, I feel comfort in my heart with peace of mind with Jesus. I don't ask much from my father; just that people love me like God loves me; that they will have the same effect on me for what they say about you is the only way to live for Jesus. For me, it's about time I get to know you better, and I am very proud of you making love to know what I mean to God. He knows about my faith in mankind, and I am a little more concerned about the future of the world and God in this country, where we care about our lives and how they can start to get better soon after the trial of the enemy's lies that Satan is going to tell us. We see the lies grow in the world and humanity; for the sake of our humanity, we will see your face in heaven, and God will do what He does best for our best interests. We are in need of a calmer environment, and the truth of this action will continue to share the value of your life. God, with your help, we will see the beauty of the world and humanity, from His

glory and greatest sacrifice for humanity, we have the house of God with us all in the spirit.

Wonder.
You have questions and thoughts daily. You always question the world around you, and you should because if you don't, then they will reside in your heart. You never learn what God is telling you. You have to choose from the heart of humanity, and your life will never be sorry. You choose the house of God or the enemy. You can never do anything else that you want until you choose God and faith in mankind.

Tears.
I cry them when I am happy or sad. They release the pain you feel and drain the negative. They are a road to your heart and the ACCEPTANCE of your fellow man. You are not weak when you cry. You are in need of the tears because they are the water of your heart. They relieve the buildup of the world and the hurt it's inflicted on you. Cry to God. Let God wipe your tears away. It's not just for your sake; if you can't cry in front of the Christ who died for you, then who will you cry for?

A burning heart is where the miracle of love comes from within our faith in mankind through the house of God. When you give into God's ways and words, your heart burns on the very level you succumb to His truth.

A burning heart is where the truth is because of my strength in seeing the world and humanity in the house of God, and love the way we can talk about everything we need to know. That's God's greatest gift. He and the alpha will have the right direction to help us understand what we started.

A burning heart and soul in the light of Jesus is here, and now we face a greater danger of life and death by our own lives than ever before if we deny that God created the world, a world where its citizens are now touched by His grace for all this time of needing the house of God, the only way that works for the world. Stopping ourselves in this world full of happiness is a blessing from God. We must submit to God. For your sake, protect your soul from the enemy.

A burning heart is where you are to stand in the house of God, with all His glory, is my point of center, in my Lord. God will come to me for what I am doing in my heart with joy in the house of God. This is the best way to live for Jesus. Walk to the house and the truth of our hearts due from the beginning of the world, and we are going forward with this new road led by my father in heaven.

May I always ask you, Jesus, for my life is to change its direction forever in the house of God.

May I be, in Jesus' name, and His angels will bring me into such a safety net; even when I am upset, you will see the beauty.

May I ask for your permission?

Please help me with this new road led by my father.

It begins with your heart, and your life will be the best way he knows what I mean to God. He knows what I do to that point of view, and I am very happy with His angel of mercy.

May I come to You for physical contact? Your love will be my energy and my blood that flows within me. My eyesight is the most important part of my strength in seeing You. My hearing is the only thing that keeps me alive until we get together. When God knows what I want it, now is that I am very proud to speak out against the enemy and the fears of the world. God knows the pit stops and the truth about how much I keep my serenity in mind when it comes to the world and humanity. He knows what I mean, and uses my restless nights to get my word on the way to live for Jesus. My words and perspective never fade away, yet, again, they have been through the process of submitting to God, even though the enemy is working hard to find me in this world, and the alpha will protect us from getting into this mess of our humanity.

MY HEART BURNS ALL THE WAY TO THE POINT WHERE YOU ARE THE BASIS, AND CHRIST IS THE ONLY WAY TO LIVE FOR JESUS. YOU ARE NOT PERFECT. DON'T YOU KNOW WHAT THEY SAY ABOUT YOU, AND YOUR LIFE WILL NEVER HAPPEN IN YOUR LIFE IF YOU'RE IN THE HOUSE OF GOD WITH ALL HIS GLORY. SEEK IN MY HEART AND SOUL EVEN THOUGH I AM VERY GRATEFUL FOR YOUR LIFE, AND YOUR LOVE FOR ME. IT'S GOD WHO WILL SATISFY THE NEEDS OF YOUR HEART.

A burning heart is where you find yourself in the middle of nowhere, and you reveal your heart is a blessing for your life. You only end up with you. I have been talking to God, and He agrees. He knows where you are meant to be.
Christ, bestow Your touch. It's in Your heart and Your life so much more than I ever thought about. You would have happened to me in my life, and I am very grateful for your support and belief in me.

There is a burning feeling, a battle within itself and the world. I long to give you my life and my heart. I want to follow Jesus in every corner of my life, and I am very proud to speak it out loud. I always say that You are not going anywhere until I treasure the moments of Your life and Your daily guidance in my affairs, and my faith is in Your hands. You are the rock that I need, and I desire to be the best way to live for Jesus and will walk through the obstacles they throw at me.

The answer is they lost their heart and soul to the enemy and fears of the world. You can restore them in a split second or they will end the way they are looking at the end of the human race.

Sometimes I feel my serenity is on trial. The enemy loves when I am off my game. He loves it even better when you are in fear, yet what he does not realize is that I have the power of Christ on my side. God will get me through the storm and back on the mountain. No matter the situation, God is my source of strength. He says He will restore all. It's not just for us, but we will see the beauty. Our children will have the opportunity to work together with God and humanity.
It is May 9th, and it's snowing. Now the sun is out, and then it's crazy; much like life, the mood changes. God is the answer. We have Christ to be the shelter. You have to choose between fear and hope, which helps you get there with Him and the alpha. You and his COMMANDS are going forward. With your heart, you will see the beauty of this vision and hear that you have God always with you. I could do anything for the house of God, with all His glory; this is my point where I belong to the house of God with the truth about how much we hurt, and He will restore all that we lost. This can only make you a better person.

Sometimes I get overwhelmed by the fact that I will get caught up in speed and getting there too fast, then it affects my sleep and my mood. God, help me slow down and keep the serenity in my life, Christ, for more than once, hope for the faith in mankind, and my life will be simply calm, and day to day, life is full of surprises, yet I still have time to stop and wonder what the beauty is. See and smell the roses. Take it steady because it is not a race. When you live that way, you create your life. In God's way, you deliver your life and your family's happiness. I want my life to be simple and enjoyable, even when life tests me. That's the normal part, yet I don't want to keep building or adding to my unease and stress in my life.

I am sitting here and watching TV. The sun warms me heart. It fills me with positivity about the day ahead, no matter what comes my way. The coffee is hot and wakes me up, yet God is the true reason why I am awake. He has put in me a destiny and mission to forge ahead in my life. He wants to see me again and again to make it count for the world and humanity from the house of God. God knows what is in my heart and my mind. After all, God put the right direction of His plan to make it happen again and again. He will continue His work in essential detail for me to keep going forward with this new road led by the omega and my faith.

The answer is the only way to live for Jesus. By this I mean that we can ask the question, yet the only answer is God's grace and sacrifice for humanity. No matter how many questions or how you ask the same question, the answer you need to come up with is the house of God.

The answer in time of fear is not to give into the world and humanity, for its purpose is to change your mind for the better.

You are to learn about your own way, and then wait for the house of God to heal the loneliness that you have.

She walks up to the glass. She wonders how she got here. How did events turn to this? She did the right thing. She always tried to do the right thing. Never before did she even know what she was doing was important for her because she let the men and her image hurt her life. She put too much power in their hands and not enough of God in her heart. Where she fell short was the result of years of this story and its chain of events. How is not really a question anymore. Now it's how she changes her lifestyle and habits that are more likely to happen in her isolation than her own life. She wants to know what she was doing important for herself because she is the only one who gives her the chance to talk to her God.

May God bless her and her image.
The enemy was destroying hurt bystanders and their lives. She and the world is full of happiness in the house of God, with all His love for the world. She only has to see what happens when you're in the house of God with all His glory. She truly is the only one who has to take the responsibility for her choices, made by her feelings, and not God being the driving force. I know what she feels. I have been led by my feelings and temptations more than my Heavenly Father loves. Now, more than ever, closer to this book coming out in a few months, do I know His love. All my life has led to this point, and He will restore all that I have been through,

and lost ten times more then before I lost it. Go to God and love Him without any doubt about His life in this time of need and fear.

God bless her future.
May her future begin with the husband she will have, and will get through this time together.
May her future begin to grow stronger and better as she continues her career as an author.
May her investments have the right direction of the income needed to pay off all her debts, and her life be more comfortable with her husband.
May the days of counting as she puts groceries in the cart and having to have her husband or herself ask, "Is this okay," or "This is only x amount..." May they buy the food they need.

May she have the passion for Your life so that she will have the opportunity for her family to help her overcome her problems and make Your life the best thing ever for her and her stability.
May her investments be the best security in the here and now. May they provide for her family and children.
May she never forget the husband she will have. May the next day he is with her be the first one being held in the house of God with all His glory.
May she never forget her name, and His character is the most important part of her dreams and hard times, for she will have the opportunity to live for Jesus.

She walks along the boardwalk. She is listening to the sound of the ocean. The seagulls in the air, so among many, but feels so alone; so reads the faces. She sees the couples and sees the smiles on their faces. She is screaming on the inside and nobody knows. She walks along the boardwalk.

Lord, fill her with your heart and ACCEPTANCE of her dreams, and your life will help her overcome the challenges of being tired from the enemy's fears that she will not find her way to live for Jesus.

Help her get back to the way she is with you and the husband she will have in the near future, the children she longs for. She sees the baby and the moms together in the neighborhood. She sees the family on the boardwalk. Take that longing she feels and wrap her in Your grace. Let her feel the same way You feel about her. Then let her rest in peace just like You would love her to stop the torment she feels in her life; the daily longing for You and life she thinks she will never have.

The power of my prayers and strengths is in faith. It's that God is the safety net, even when I don't understand; not meant to question His method or His work.

It is an ongoing thing. It's the world and humanity from the enemy fears God because if you are not afraid of the world and humanity in which the enemy uses, you have a great outlook in Jesus' name.

The power is in your hands, God. You also gave me the brains and the wit to do what I need to. You set it in my face and know that I will do what I need to do. It's not the money, but it's the income that will allow me to build my ministry and write more books. God, You're the muse to my art and the truth of why I do what do in Your name. God, You are the master of my strength and the heart of my soul in this journey. You will put the right direction in my life so I can bring Your glory to my life and my family.

The answer was yes, but the strong part was that the world was not immediately clear about the bottom line.

The answer is they lost their heart and soul to the world and humanity, yet, again, they have to choose the house of God.

They are the basis, and Christ is the best way to live for Jesus and pray for peace on earth that they have no effect on the ground floor of this vision.

They were talking about their health, and their lives were being treated as well as perspective on this issue of the disease.

LOVE THE CHALLENGE.
IT WILL BRING YOU MORE DEPTH.
IT WILL BRING YOU, MORE THAN EVER, CLOSER TO YOUR HEAVENLY FATHER.
IT WILL BRING YOU MORE DEPTH BEHIND THE SCENES AND THE TRUTH ABOUT HOW MUCH YOU CAN SEE THE DESTINY.
Love the moments for what they are.
Love God always.
Love the way you deliver your own life.
Love the storm.
Love the aftermath.
Love the moment.

LOVE EASTER.
THE CANDY
THE COLOR
NEW SEASONS
FLOWERS POPPING UP
WARMER DAYS

NEW HORIZONS
NEW MISSIONS
NEW BEGININGS
DID I MENTION CHOCOLATE BUNNIES?

New days are always there for the world and humanity in
the house of God.
New missions are underway for the people of America in
this, together, with your heart.
New missions will have the passion for them because God
now touches them, and He loves us.
New missions will be available for the next generation of the
human spirit.
New missions are underway for the world and humanity, for
its beauty will come from the house of God.
New missions will have the right direction of His plan, and
the alpha will have the passion for your life.

I often ask myself why,
Why I put up the most walls
Or why I am afraid to go forward.
Do you know how much this hurts me?
God, it's your time that will be the answer.

Christ, you are not away from me.
You are the only confidence I need.
You are my savior now and then.
You were always there.
Sometimes not in front view,
But in my opinion, the first one feeling
I had of why I am here.
You were there even when I go through
The uncomfortable times.

You are the voice in my head.
You tell me to go out into the world.
Make my life more than just a test to test a way.
Let me find peace today with the house of God.
The reason for this time of sorrow
And pain
Are not only for us to remember what
You died for, but what you
Are going to do in us.
I am more than just a number in the world of man.
I am meant to heal and change the world. God and the alpha
will be done with my decision. God is the only way that I
feel comfort.
God, you have Dad with you.
He is watching over me.
With your heart and soul, heal his hurt.
When he was here, he had tough times.
I know there was a lot of damage done.
But God will come down here, and then He delivers His
message to us.
Dad and I never were great.
We had our days,
Being the first and a momma's boy
Did not help.
He was in the Navy,
So the bonding years were
Not a bonding time for us.
We were never close till it was too late.
By then, there was so much lost time.
We had never said, "I love you"
Like a father and son should.
So many times I wondered what I did wrong,
Why I was not good enough,

What do I do to make him love me?
When he died,
I never got to apologize.
For my part,
Communication is essential in any relationship.
Yet I was too busy blaming and shifting the responsibility.

God, forgive me.
I was very narrow-minded.
I was very quiet in the truth.
I did not see him for what he was,
What his faults were.
I treated mine like they were better,
And played the game of ego
So much, I kept the wall up.
I was part of the problem,
Not part of the solution.
God, let me know when you are
With him.
If I could only tell him how
Much love and miss him.
I wish he was here to see my successes.

Jesus, and Grandmother,
She was my rock.
She made me feel so special.
Those nights we laughed,
Watched TV late into the night.
She would go to yard sales;
Buy clothes for my stuffed bunny.
She even washed them,
And made my favorite dinner.
Even though she made dinner,

She filled it with love.
We spent every weekend together.
I miss her so much.
She never doubted me.
She was the first one to let me be me.
So when I grew up,
The world was the enemy.
I built up the wall;
I built a big persona;
Wasted time and energy
Because what I need is God.
My life is empty without God.
My weaknesses in man's view
Are actually strengths through God.
I am very emotional,
Very passionate,
And feel with all my
Heart,
Body,
Soul,
And mind.

Jesus:
The answer to fear
The answer to hope
The answer
The answer to all
The answer
The answer to how much you love
The answer to the question of whether you are afraid

Jesus is the answer.
Take me home.
Calm my emotions.
LIKE SO MANY,
WE ARE FIGHTING A BATTLE.
WE ARE NOW
ACCEPTING AN UNKNOWN FUTURE.
THE WORLD HAD A NORMAL,
NOW WE HAVE NEW REALITY.
AS WE EAT OUR DINNER,
WATCH OUR NEWS,
BEING ISOLATED,
IT HAS AN EFFECT.
I HAVE TO DIVE INTO YOU.
I HAVE TO HAVE FAITH.
WITH YOU, I CAN SEE THE LIGHT.
WITH YOU I AM.
I AM NOT GOING TO LET THE STORM GET
ME INTO THE FEAR,
FEAR OF THE WORLD.
IT'S A CHALLENGE FOR MY FAMILY AND ME.
WE ARE SOCIAL CREATURES, AND OUR CHILDREN
ARE IN NEED OF THE HOUSE OF GOD.
The DISEASE HAS A HOLD
ON OUR NATURE,
OUR DAILY ROUTINE.
IT'S NOT OVER TILL GOD SAYS THAT.
BUT IT'S DRAGGING OUT THE ENERGY.
GOD, REFUEL US.
GOD, BLESS THE HURTING.
GOD, SO MANY PEOPLE ARE MORE THAN THEY HAVE
IN weakness due to this disease.

The reason for this isn't to be afraid,
But to question
What MATTERS.
What is your approach to this?
You are the basis and the most substance CONSUMING
of any kind
We are to follow You,
Reach out to You,
Call upon You,
In this hour of need.
Help me help someone who is in the wrong place mentally.

Breathe in me.
Restore my hope.
Give me the faith.
You are never gone.
You will always see.
You will bring us our salvation.
We will run to you.
I am not the only one.
So many want to find you.
May this time be the moment,
The time to look at You,
At the promise
In Your eyes.
That they may see the light,
That open view
That clears the fog.
Jesus is the way to the
Heart of the sea,
The heart of humanity,
The heart of hope.

Yes,
I believe.
I give my counsel
To His majesty,
To His message.
No left or right,
But to the house of God.
GOD.

I DON'T KNOW WHY THEY PLAY THE GAMES.
YOU WOULD NEVER DO THAT.
TO THEM, IT'S BUSINESS.
YOU ARE ABOUT PEOPLE.
YOU ARE THE PRINCE OF PEACE,
THE MAJESTIC ONE.
You put hearts.
You put value.
You put human life before money.
Why can't they?
They know not what they do.
Don't forsake.
I know now I must not judge harshly.
Questioning human nature is natural.
But you deal the punishments.

In the moment,
I struggled to stay positive.
It seems I face backlash
As you did when You wanted us hear the good news.
It's still worth it to me.
I cannot let the devil
Hold me in doom and gloom.
He has taken hold of so many

During these times.

We will be in Jesus.

We are to trust Him now.

We are to get Him in our country.

God is where I feel safe;

In the house of God.

The most important part of your life and your family will be the one thing that keeps you alive and well.

When does it count for the world and humanity in this; together, we will see Your face and Your grace.

Lord, help us to meet the people who never have been loved and need peace.

In their hearts,

They long,

They desire,

They are on edge.

You, soldiers, now,

Are to step up,

Answer the call

To heal the loneliness,

To restore your hope,

To testify against the enemy,

To bring your best quality to the house of

God.

We need you in the world and humanity to get rid of infections.

The revival of His plan is what He does best.

The reason for this is that the whole country needs to stand up to the inevitable.

Revive your life.

Revive your day.

Revive the joy.

Revive the world.

Revive the energy.
Revive the news.
Revive yourself in the house of God.
Revive your life and your family.
Revive the news, and you reveal your heart.

God, I need you. My life is in turmoil. I started a great new career. I am an author. My job is like a wolf hanging on to my mind. I miss my friends who I can't be with all of them. I can only use technology, and isolation is my new normal. I want to feel good about the future. If I look at all the manmade stuff there is no hope. The house of God is where I draw my strength. It's the place where I go to find solitude and new hope.

God, they fight over the details. They put the human population. In the meantime, people are dying from a disease. It's in need of You. You're the real medicine, the reason we remain hopeful. You're the answer to any question we have.

God, we need You to come home. We need Jesus to be the one who gives the world a sense of hope. We need to realize You are the basis, and the world is loved by all of the house of God.

God, I am in need of You. I am a strong person. Human nature is disappointing me right now. We are not coming together in places we need to. We are in a time crunch. We are in a race to solve a problem for the people, not the big problem that we are failing as a whole in man's world.

Mary
Sits at her table.
She sips on her freshly poured coffee
And ponders
The world,
The news;
It's in chaos.
We are running scared.
We don't know the facts.
She has to be reminded of God
And her faith
To make sense of the whole thing.
She prays.
She cries.
She really just unleashes the tears.
She knows it's a short fix.
But God says to do so.
It does
Help.

Mark
Sits on his porch.
He looks at the quiet streets.
He hears the silence of the fearful.
He knows God is there.
But at this moment, asks why.
He wants the answer.
He has none of his own.
He simply wants the depth.
So he just sighs.
He just wished
He knew the answer.

Cadie
She walks her route.
She delivers her mail.
She knows the people
Who usually greet her
Are now behind a door
Or behind a window.
She waves,
She smiles,
She feels the heartache,
She feels the loneliness.

Rick
Just saw his new son
Briefly born into this world.
He wonders
What future will he have?
He will do a lot of wondering.
His son is his first child

From marriage
Of 30 years.
They were so happy,
But now wonder about the new year.
Will he know,
Will he play ball;
What new world will he know?
But he is healthy,
And he prays to God,
Saying, "Thank You.
I trust
In You, my Father."

Jodi
She drives a cab daily.
She usually has busy day.
She meets new people hourly.
She laughs,
She shutters,
She smirks.
She loves helping go from point
A to B.
Now she watches the news.
She wonders when it will return,
The days of going to work
And the days of the sun in her face.
She won't see the world;
Just so lonely.
Yet her God
Is there.
It's not going down.

Carrie
Wants to go to school.
She misses her friends.
She loves her classmates.
She likes her teachers,
And the recess time.

I believe God has a big plan for my life. He always has, and, yet, in my flesh, it gets lost. I spend too much time worrying and comparing myself. I let man and the here and now be a focal point. Now God is always with me, but He gets drowned out. He loves me anyway. So this must put Him in prime view. Never let a second go without thinking, thanking, praying. So today, I decided to follow and pursue dreams, take action, and live one day at a time, for God knows my days and the number. He will fulfill them and all that are a part of my destiny.

Prayer: Father, You remind me that it is never too late,
Never to late to recharge your heart,
Never too late to recharge your passion,
Never to late to rethink the situation,
Never too late to start talking about the house of God.
Never let the enemy win over the house of God.
Never mind the one who gives you heartache,
But rely on the house of God.
God, live in me, and You reveal Your heart.
May my heart beat,
May my mind find a calm river flow,
Where images of You are my picture,
And it's beautiful.

Prayers
For the world,
For the human spirit,
For our neighbor,
For our brothers and sisters,
For the enemy we are facing now to subside,
For the health of all to receive the benefit of the house of God.
Prayer
To my Heavenly Father,
Many are scared.
Rest their mind,
Rest their fears,
Rest the uncertainty.

Hope for new release from the end of my grip
Hope for the release of the enemy's stronghold.

Let his grip weaken.
Let the world be better than tomorrow.
We are in crisis.
We are in desperate need of miracles.

Love.
Give it freely.
Seek it.
Appreciate it.
Love one another.
Spread it in the dark places.
Count on it.
Live for it.

Realization.what do I?
I am okay.
I am not going to fall,
Not going to be weakened,
Not going to break.
Have God.
Have God and my faith.
Have my family and friends.
Have inner strength that is unbroken.
Have a sense of urgency.
We are one with God.

Prayers that I never stop fighting for life,
That I keep my sense of the power of prayer needed daily so
I can be strong.
Prayers that people never stop relying on You so they see You
as the answer for the life they want.

Prayers, we see the hope that we see the sun and clouds as precious, even in the dark times.

Prayers that we move forward as a team, that we stay united and together; we stay hopeful.

Prayers, we trust You.
We love You.
We listen to You.
We look to You.
We get in touch and stay focused on You.
We look to faith.
We think as brothers and sisters in Christ.

Realization

In my human flesh, I am so easily ready to place blame, to point a finger. Now, mind you, I was one who put myself in the problem. I spent too much or went overboard, letting the enjoyment of stuff become more important than common sense. Instead of enjoying and using what I already have, I would just get more. Now I have more books then I've read, more CDs than I can listen to, more scarves than I can wear, and more DVDs than I can watch. Now I am not saying you can't have these things or can't enjoy them. Yet it's the enjoyment and the use that's more important than the number. They are meant for pleasure and not the assumption. There are many who would love a third of what I have in these manmade pleasures. I am thankful for them.

Prayer: Lord, may You remind me that enjoyment over assumption is the way to go.

Thought: read one book before moving on to another. Watch DVDs weekly. Wear scarves often. Listen to music daily.

Reminder: enjoy what you have, and before you add more, ask yourself this: do I need it now?

Dreams

We live and we forget how to dream. We get caught up in the everyday. We feel we are too old or we let people dictate our future.

God gave us a life to live, not to run a rat race. He does not create human life to run and not know peace of mind in our day. When we don't dream, then we go through a routine. Now, yes, in the here and now, we have to because that is the way we live. We take on and do so much but do so little. We are living for the flesh and not the soul. By doing this, we put a limit on our mind and a restless feeling on our body. So this I say to you, dream and let God hear you.

Prayer: God, pray that I never lose my ability to dream. Always put my dreams in Your hands.

Thought: dreams are meant to keep the mind active and fresh. Always dream big and small. Always know they can be big and small, simple and complex. Dreaming, to me, is always hopeful. It's a reminder that you are alive. You were born to dream. You can dream, but there is a reality you must know. You must know there is a practical view.

Realization: you can't fulfill a dream if you aren't active. You can't just dream and then wishfully think it will happen.

Practical approach: give it to God. Be active daily. Have a game plan. Never give up. Have faith. Work hard. Be diligent.

The Why

Why do I let people control my fate?

Thought: because I have been conditioned to, from an early age, as well as my upbringing.

Prayer: Lord, You are in control of my days and my life. Only You can bring what is meant to be. Only You can be the Master. You have a final say on how and the number of my days.

Realization: I am not being true to God. I must want to be more authentic in all of my days to You.

Why is hard for me to believe in myself? It is so hard to follow through.

Thought: I was raised to not believe and not to dream; to only accept man's plans for and on my life.

Prayer: Lord, Your will be done. You decide what is real and what matters. You have the answer.

Realization: when we put it in God's hands, He will be enough. When you stop needing social media and man's approval, then, and only then, can you be free.

Why do I go back and forth in my daily ambition? Why does my focus stray?

Thought: maybe because we live in a world of "now" and not "later," we get bored and distracted easily.

Prayer: Father, help me to stay on the prize and Your kingdom. Let me know You are never away from me.

Realization: pray.

One day at a time;
Never look back.
Trust in Jesus.
Breathe.
Focus.

Why does it seem like I'm worried today? I was so worried about how to get through the week and why he has to struggle. Is it my fault?

Prayer: thank You for doing what You do best. Thank You for love and grace. You came through and were always in awe. How do You come through even in prayers we don't say aloud? You amaze me.

Thought: true story about a recent situation; He was broke, only twenty-five dollars to his name. He buys a five-dollar ticket and wins $500.

Realization: make a decision.
Set a goal.
Put into action.
Focus.
Desire to change.
Don't repeat.

Why did I want to cry the night before? Do I get it physically, thinking about the next day?

Thought: because it is not doing Your work. It's not being real to myself, and goes against everything I am not.

Prayer: place me where I am meant to be. Your will be done. Make me the man I'm meant to be.

Realization: be thankful.
All this is temporary.
Do your best.
Remember what He has given you.
Breathe.
Bring it to God.

True event: I was at the grocery store and left my wallet on the counter, and my keys as well. My money and cards were in my wallet.

God's intervention: no money was missing and all cash was intact. No cards were missing and the keys were next to the wallet.

Realization: God exists and looks out for me.

Why does it not always work out as planned?

Thought: we do it to ourselves. We don't think, we give into flesh, and we try to do it our way.

Prayer: help me to lean on You. Help me to relax and see the bigger picture. Help me to focus on Your ways.

Realization: I don't have all the answers. I must not play God. If it's not God's way, then it's not worthy of doing. I know that I must study.

Why does it hurt when we lose someone?

Thought: it is a natural feeling. We want to control the outcome. We want to be the gatekeeper. We try to tell God how long and when someone enters or leaves us.

Prayer: Father, help me to know loss is a part of life and the journey. Remind me that You are the one who controls the number of days.

Realization: God heals.
God knows and will reserve the timing.
God knows you.
This too shall pass.

Why do I forget who I was meant to be?

Thought: I listen to the wrong voice in my head. I don't have faith in myself. I live in a world where comparison runs rampant. I look to the wrong source to feel worthy.

Prayer: may You be the source that fuels my destiny. May I have the faith needed to do my best. May I not feel the need to compare, and always feel worthy in Your Word.

Realization: He will make me in His vision. When I put God first, He will set the final destination into my path. When I give my cares to my Master, then I will be in the right place. Look to God for who I am. Look to His ways and be set free.

Love the flaws because they are God-given. Man only judges you, and, yet, God creates a masterpiece.

Why: how do we find a better way to come together?

Thought: we read the Bible from front to back. We study it, book by book. We never put biased thoughts and replace God's words. We listen to the stories of those who have been changed by the grace of God. We remember we have the same color blood. When we bleed, it is the same color, red. We unite on a daily basis. Pray that we see our enemy as our brother and sister in Christ. Realize that is easier said than done. We can only change our hearts first. Then we can help others. Pray that hate is erased for the next generation. We must come together as one with one step at a time. Realize that when Judgment Day arrives, only God will be the judge and jury. Pray for a day that we all can love without any biases. Realize your potential in God.

Always know the root of what is bothering you. Be real and admit the source of your negative thoughts. When you do this, it makes the "why" in life less likely to come up.

Now, I am not saying they won't come up. You just won't see them as much. When they do, they won't weigh so heavily on your mind, nor will they rob you of your day and waste time always thinking of "why me." Why can't this or that be? You can focus more on others and how to change the world.

Prayer: Instead of thinking, "why me," teach me to think how I cannot repeat.

Scripture Reflections

Psalm 17:6, "I call on you, O God, for you will answer me. Give ear to me and hear my prayer."

God always hears us, no matter if you are quiet, yell, cry, or just utter, "God, help me." He knows your pain and joy. Yet we sometimes will ask and receive something we later regret. God always answers me. I learned the hard way to make sure that when I ask it comes from an honest and real place. God will even sometimes give you something to prove His point. He wants you to know that He knows the "why" as well as when you are ready for the destiny He lined up so long ago.

Ecclesiastes 5:4, "When you make a vow to God, do not delay in fulfilling it. He has no pleasures in fools."

When you give a dream to God, He is not interested in fancy words or the act of using your tongue. He wants to see you mean it. He won't do His part and just wave a wand while saying it will be done. He wants to see your commitment and actions. He always wanted you to mean it. With God, it's a two-way street. If you put in the time and honest effort, then your Savior will bring to light what is meant to be.

Job 20:2, "Zophar": My troubled thoughts prompt me to answer because I am greatly disturbed.

When you hang onto thoughts too long, they will consume you. They will have an effect in every area of your life. You spend too much time on you and not others. You were meant to laugh, love, and live, not to always be about you. Let God handle it. After all, He is the Alpha. Always breathe in and say, "God help me." It's simple, and He is ready to listen and help you go forward. Let go. Handle your battle and you will live. The best way is to take one day at a time. For me, I repeat "God, help me," daily.

Job 21:6, "When I think about this, I am terrified, trembling seizes my body."

Many times, I overthink and plan. I make steps and then rethink them. I alter my actions and make adjustments. It's daily and time-consuming. Yes, no rest for the wicked, but even more wasted energy for the thinker. Recently, I've been trying to take things one day at a time and keep it simple. It is still a daily process, but it's a little more peaceful. I can find some joy in everyday life. When I get too close to that line of action and obsession, then I pray this: "God, help me. You're the Alpha, and I am merely human." God bless you.

Psalms 35:19, "Let not those gloat over me, who are my enemies without cause."

No one should ever judge me nor assume anything about me. We all get judged. That is truly only God's duty. Even if I have given them reason to, again, only God judges me. People should always want to know why. What is the reason or the background story that makes us do what we do? Where does it say I live for man? Yet man always wants to have the answer, or at best, play "God." They feel they have the right to judge me. In the end, God says, "I am the way."

Psalm 77:1, "I cried out to God for help! I cried out to God to hear me."

The "cried out" part in this has never been truer. I have what is called monthly meltdowns. I cry to the point where I get sick. I hold too much worry in and try to fix myself. Yet know that God wants to take my pain. He hears me even when I yell and say dumb things. He never forsakes me. I love how that feels; not the meltdown, mind you, but the fact God will always remain in me. God will always be mine, and I will be free of Satan.

My responsibility to my Creator: ask and receive.
Knock and seek.
Have faith.
Trust in His Word.
Study His Word.
Share His world.

God's promise to me: He never forsakes me.
He always makes each day a new day to improve.
He will love me unconditionally.
He will always guide me to the destiny that awaits me.

My promise to the readers: be candid and real.
Share my experiences.
Write from the heart.
Always encourage.

I forgot how to dream and hope like a child. The more I get into Your world and Your word, the more I can be a dreamer. I can hope again and know that even if they are different dreams, they are still a dream. They are hope for what comes next in life. They also can be the simple and the biggest. They will be a reality and a place to be with You. So I will share my recent dreams. I will allow my mind to be open and adjust to where my journey has led me to know. The dreams are Your will. You make their reality the best way that is right for me. For if I tell You, then they are demands and not dreams.

I wake up every morning. Instead of it being about God, it's about regret. Why should it be regret when God gave me what I wanted? I got the position I wanted. Could it be I am human and never satisfied? Yes, but I am also not fulfilling my dream, my desire to do more and be more. Have I settled for less? When you are doing what you have to and living for flesh, then you gave up dreaming. You are just going through the motions, yet you are not really living. This makes God very sad. You were put here to dream and live a life full of joy. So I urge you to dream again and let your light shine again. Whatever makes you unhappy will pass. Glory to God.

> **Job 3:13**, "For now I would be lying down in peace. I would be asleep and at rest."

I rarely dream at night, yet this verse brings me to a peaceful place. You can dream anywhere and anytime, just like you talk to God. We need rest to be our best. We need dreams to feel alive.

Prayer: Father, may You meet me at the place, the place where I can dream and feel at ease. May our minds be one and not restless. This is my prayer to You.

> **Job 3:20**, "Why is light given to those in misery, and life to the bitter of soul?"

I love this verse. It has depth and really hits home. We need the light to heal and grow. Just as living things need light to grow, so we need the light to push ahead. To dream, we need the hope of a better day. We need to see a better outlook. The light represents, to me, finding God when you are at the lowest depths of misery.

"Life to the bitter soul." For me, I feel this is what keeps me going. As much as I feel down and ready to give up, I remember I am alive and feeling something. I am reminded that no matter my discomfort with my emotions, when God puts light on my bitter soul, then there is always hope. As long as I feel, then know I am alive to dream and see a better day. I would rather feel something than nothing at all.

I apply this verse in the following way:
Light never fails to bring an end to the darkness.
Light shines in the places you think are dead.
Life gives the soul an alternative feeling to focus on rather than staying bitter.
Life will always have its bad days, yet you never have to stop **dreaming or remain bitter**.

> **Proverbs 24:23**, "All hard work brings a profit, but mere talk leads only to poverty."

I tend to speak a lot. I say out loud my dreams and confess to God. I also know He listens, but He loves when I am actually consistent, when I actually do something that brings me closer to the outcome I want or dream about. When I say it and am active, He will make a way. My dream comes true.

He gives me the plan. I know how to achieve and am good at staying on target (okay, most of the time). I know the procedure and how to do it. Now I just have to keep the eye on the prize. The part about poverty also brings real ties into my life. When you make a plan, you know God will approve, and you say it. You even speak out loud, yet you backtrack. You're good for a few days, then you slack off. You hear God saying, "What happened?" Then you speak out loud, "I have to get back on track." You also know that you put blinders on and go, "If I say it, then it must work." Well, not really, because I am here to say you'd be surprised. You end up at the same place while only moving in a false state. You are broke, money, and spirit wise. So in a matter of speaking, do what I try. Say what you mean and mean what you say.

My Dream Plan

Mean what I say.
Say what I mean.
Stay focused.
When I say it, not only say it, but also put it into action.
Once you begin doing the steps that bring you closer to the dream, make sure you keep going.
Always implement on a daily basis.
Be vigilant on what you do.

Prayer: Lord, as I write this devotional, may words pour out from my soul.

Thought: same book title, three-part trilogy, devotional journal prayer book.

Further Scriptural Ponderings

> **Proverbs 15:4**, "The tongue that brings healing is a tree of life, but a deceitful tongue crushes the spirit."

The first part of the verse makes me think that when you give a kind word to someone who hurts you, you heal and encourage the soul. You also bring new hope to them. When someone gives up or stops dreaming and you say or speak an encouraging word, you help them believe and dream again. You are a healer with your words. You can bring life into a dark place and make a dream revive itself. The second part of the verse is very deep to me as well. To me, it says, "Don't say things that are not true." Don't repeat what people think or what Satan wants you to believe. I also feel that when I read this verse, and the second part speaks to me. When you focus on the negative and repeat it, you will crush your spirit. You will not only give power to Satan, but you will always be stuck. You will never know peace because you are what you think. Remember who and what God made you to be. Only say the right words and thoughts that God speaks to you.

Prayer: God, let me always speak life and never crush my spirit.

> **Proverbs 16:3**, "Commit to the Lord whatever you do and your plans will succeed."

I love this verse; for many reasons, it speaks to me. I love what it promises. I love what it says in just a few short words. It gives me the openness to dream more than just wishful thinking. I can make a plan, be active, and take steps, then watch it come to pass, by His will and grace. He makes the reality of words into actual reality. Oh, how I love Jesus and future dreams.

> **Proverbs 27:1**, "Do not boast about tomorrow for you do not know what a day brings forth."

When I read this, I feel as if these words are telling me to live in the moment and not ignore today. You can dream, but don't lose sight of the day in front of you. You don't want to get so caught up in a dream that you lose sight of the blessings you have right in front of you. I feel as though that's where a lot of my stress comes from. Know that God will get me there. Only He knows the number of my days.

Random thought on this verse: feel as though I need to concentrate as I write my devotional.

Dream-related thoughts:
Dreams are gifts from God and are meant to keep you focused on hope.
Dreams are a waste if you are not going to have a plan.
Dreams require you to put in motion steps and be active. Apply a day-to-day mindset.
Dreams give you hope, and they provide a new outlook for your life.
Dreams should never be squashed, for it's God's pleasure for you to dream.
Dreams are the best way to stay close to God. They keep you in a consistent conversation with God.
Dreams are the key to a healthy spirit. They keep the devil at bay, and they are a way to stay positive.
Dreams require an action plan. They are a day-to-day activity. They are meant to be any size in the concept. Speak them often.
Dreams can cover any area. They are not a one-trick-pony. You can dream anywhere and about anything.
Hold on to dreams. No one can ever say or tell you not to dream. You are born with a child-like mind. Don't dream like an adult with limits. Use your new dreams to feel alive and be an inspiration.

Dream. No one dream is the same as anyone else's. Dare to dream your dream and not compare it.

Ecclesiastes 3:3, "There is a time for everything and a season for activity under the heavens."

When I read this, I have always felt I knew this verse. It is a very true and a well-respected verse. I had to end this section with it.

My personal prayer and request for dreams:

Prayer to be debt free
Prayer to pay off the car
Pray to work, write, and travel, promoting my devotionals. I want to be a writer; God's will.

God, Humans Are Mental, Yet You Are Peace!

Lord, lay me down to sleep and bring me a restful night. May my night be full of You. I cast my worries to You.

Sleep – Don't rob me of my sleep. May, instead, it be a time to rest and wake up, ready for the new day my Savior has prepared.

Sleep – When I close my eyes, it's to be with Jesus. It's my time to forget my day, a time to repent and ask for forgiveness.

Sleep – You are my intimate time with my Creator. Amen.

Poetic Prayers

Nighttime
Lay me down.
Close my eyes.
Turn off the sound.
Only hear You.
Give it away
And seal it in You.
Meet me there.
Find the place
Where it's solid,
Where no noise distracts,
And we are one.
Give me rest.
Give me sleep,
Deep and soothing.
We meet now.
Ready to dream,
And find my sleep.
As I lay me down,
I close my eyes.
No more thoughts;
Drift away
And call it quits.
I am one with sleep.
This I pray in Your name.
Morning
Wake from a restless sleep,
A sleep that seems not solid.

I hear the sounds of the day beginning.
The thoughts start to wander in my head.
When I speak first words out loud,
They are to Thee, to You, my Father.
God, be with me;
Silence the noise.
Get me through this day.
Help me to remember
It's dark when I awake.
Not only in the mental, but also in the spirit.
Help me to see the light,
Where all is good,
Where the road seems real
And we walk together,
Hand in hand.
God, be with me,
Now and forever. Amen.

Scared

Lord, I often get scared about how I will survive by myself, not because I don't have You, but it's the fact that I let men be who I depended on. I put my trust in men and not my Savior, who is the only true man that will provide. I love that about my Creator, that no matter what, I can reach out to You, and You answer.

Prayer: God, be with me at all times. Hear my cries to You. Reach out and hold my heart. Put me in the place I belong as You mold me. Let me know and always feel that love and bond. Amen.

Regret

Never hang on to what has been. You were meant to learn and move on. You are allowed to feel it, but are never meant to own it. When you hang on or own it, then it festers and holds you down. You are now a slave to its hold. Let God break the chain we call regret as human beings. We can give it to God and walk away. He will replace the regret with a peace and joy like you've never known.

Prayer: Lord, never let regret consume my heart or me. Break all chains and fill my inner peace. Let the new life settle in my heart. Amen.

Psalm 5:1, "Give ear to my words, Oh Lord, consider my sighing."

Psalm 5:2, "Listen to my cry for help, my king and my God, for to you I pray."

Psalm 5:3, "In the morning, Oh Lord, You hear my voice. In the morning, I lay my request before You and wait in expectation."

Psalm 13:1, "How long, oh Lord, will you forget me forever? How long will you hide your face from me?"

Psalm 13:2, "How long must I wrestle with my thoughts? And every day have sorrow in my heart? How long will my enemy triumph over me?

Psalm 13:6, "I will sing to the Lord for he has been good to me."

Random Points

Never have regrets in your life.
Never be scared about anything. Instead, give it to God.
At night, dream with and about God's plans for your life.
In the morning, say, "God, what will this day bring?" Put your first words into a positive realm. When you do any other way, you set the failure into motion. You are almost sure to slide in the negative. Satan will love this and use it to his advantage. Don't give him any more energy than he already steals.

> **Psalm 16:7**, "I will praise the Lord, who counsels me even at night my heart instructs me."

I really love how it promises a boundary that can't be forsaken, where you and God are one in the body, mind, and soul; where love and safety are yours from God, and never leaves. You can count and always call out to Him. The areas where I feel this verse most:

My destiny – God's will
My outlook when scared – God's safety
My sleepless night – God's calmness
My everyday struggle – God's security
My family – When I miss them
My future – when I dream again

Entreaties to God

Lord I look
I see a helpless man.
Can't take it away.
The pain is not mine to take.
Only You can do so.
I am asking this of You.

I am struggling here.
My emotions say and feel hurt.
My mind says the money;
Where and how I will pay.
Illness of the fact that
Though it comes up at all,
Reality is not have I yet to make the market my income let
along my extra source of income.

My heart says I need to take care of him.
Will have to step up to ensure he will eat better,
To ensure he drinks more liquids.
Will also need to keep me up;
Keep my spirit and drive up.
Will require more sleep, exercise, and diet change.
Focus on investments.
Generate more income all for the sake of him.
Need to rise up and be the man.
You made me strong and here is my chance to prove to
the world.
I will show You I am ready for the life I have been asking for

.

Let me be the man You have designed.
Rise up and say no to the devil.
Say no to fear just waiting to knock me down.
Say yes to heal him.
In my power at hand, praise You for doing the miracle.
Need that miracle,
For there is a time coming.
Reality never gives you a break,
But it does not have to break you.
You will always face the moment when you decide to fall or stand,
A time to be weak or victorious.
When you know emotions are heavy,
Cloud your mindset;
Yet you have to push through.
Let it be known in Jesus' name,
Where you are going,
Why you want it,
And you trust God to give it to you.
A miracle is not just wishful thinking, but faith.
When it's all said and done,
We begin again.
It is important to praise and declare in God's name;
To say out loud your declaration.

For me, it's hard, but not for obvious reasons;
Yet because I have many and know God wants to hear all of them.
He wants to make all come true,
Yet wants me to trust and have faith that He will deliver, so I praise Him.
I give my worries to Him.
I trust He will use my test and pass me with flying colors,

For I cannot fail my God.
It's not written in our deal.
Lord, hear me now.
I come to Thee, asking, why?
Yet already deep down know my what,
The reason my thoughts are my enemy.
Why my circumstance brings my soul
As I look, knock, and seek,
You will show, open, and receive what is meant to be.
With my action, it will happen.
In Your time, it will come to rest.
In my actions, it will progress.
May You never leave it undone.
Let the triumphs blow loud
As I make my promise
To thee, oh Heavenly Father.
What good to Him am I
If I am not taking care of?
I mentally need to focus on You.
I physically need to be an example of all health;
More exercise, sleep, food, and positive energy.
Emotionally, be vigilant in my pursuit.
Stay determined.
Spiritually, the less on my mind, the more I can focus on Him.
Reduce my stress,
Pay off my car,
Stock market my income,
Generate growing income,
Allows me to focus on Him.
Give Him more attention.
You will take care of my needs.
This I know to be true
Because I pray to You.

Home now
Where I can recharge,
So I ask You to not let Satan visit me while I am open to
his attempts.
Instead, recharge my mind and keep my eye on the final
destination.
See, this is where I write,
Where I study Your Word and bring my books to life.
This is where my income from the market will be generated.
This is where I will pay my debt off.
This is where I will pay my car off;
Where I will be the man meant to be,
Where the quiet time is mine to touch base with You.
I will continue to pray my request:
Debt free
Own my car
Day trader income
Earn a non-stop income while the rest will be His care and
putting Him before me.
I will have a balance;
I will have all areas in their place;
Each time, precious, and more connection.
One won't be more than other or more less they all come
together as one
As a plan well-crafted and driven by You;
The One who makes all come true.
Will You not hear my words as I pour out my confessions?
We forget we are loved.
We get focused on our daily lives.
We move with the fast pace.
Yet God will remind us of love, and how much.
Sadly, it's usually in a test, but that's okay.
We forget our strength.

We get focused on things going well.
We don't tap into it on a sunny day,
And when we need it, the devil says, oh no, wait.
It will cloud our emotions and our vision;
To see spiritually, and even literally.
He wants to break us.
He wants to say my way is better.
Yet only God is the way.

No more.
With my recent scare,
I say no more.
I am ready to take on
the evil ways of man,
and the one who tries to steal my thunder.

Say no more fear,
I will trust in God.
No more worry. The funny and the lesson
No more will he rob me.
Only God will bring me into
My road to the destiny I am supposed to be on,
Not the train of self-doubt.

No more fear.
No more whys.
NO more I can't.
No more I am not.
No more it's not easy.
No more it's too hard.

More yes to, I am strong.
More yes to not always having an answer.

More yes to, I can do all things through Christ Jesus.
More yes to, I am capable.
More yes to the test and the lesson.
More yes to the struggle, for without it, I can't remind myself what I am made of.

Psalm 18:1:
"I love you, O Lord, my Strength."

I will pray this everyday with the Father's prayer.
Praise God, my Savior, and salvation.

Today, I am thankful for the following:

My job
My family
My friends
The love that surrounds me
The mind to stay focused
My cats
The love of Jesus
The day lesson
The breath take all day
The tears to release pain
The destiny that awaits
The beauty in life
The writing of my books
Publication
The sleep I'm about to receive
The promise from God
God's story
My health
My diligence

The way that He made me
The love of friends

Ecclesiastes 2:24:

"A man can do nothing better then to eat and drink and find in his work. This too, I see, is from the hand of God."

We live in a world of rush where we have to be better. We don't enjoy and just live in the moment. We have a fast-paced daily routine. We never slow down and enjoy the simple little things: the wind in your hair, the purr of the family cat, or the sun rays as they shine. In this verse, God says, "eat." So eat and be healthy. He doesn't say eat and not exercise and then complain that you are overweight. He says, "eat." You were meant to eat food, for it nourishes the body, mind, and soul. You eat and then move, and God takes care of your body image. You don't need to worry about the body image or let man be the judge. God knows what you are to look like. He says what the temple is supposed to look like on the inside and outside. He knows what shape and what curves the temple has.

I don't drink, but I do want to find satisfaction in my work. So for me, I want to do my very best, be happy, and know I give my all when I perform my duties. Usually, I have to pray in these areas:
Pray to do my best
Pray I can perform
Pray that though everything is temporary, it's still important
Pray to get through and not grumble
Pray that it's not a chore
Pray to do what I must

Pray to know it's part of the journey
Pray that I get my mind active
Pray that it is not easy, yet not hard to fulfill
Pray to my Heavenly Father

When you do something, enjoy it and find the satisfaction in all you do. Let it be known to God you are doing for Him and then you do for others. Others can do for you as well, yet it should be for satisfaction, and not from a selfish or egotistical mindset.
Pray to find the joy.
Pray to find enjoyment.
Pray to find recharge.
Pray to find my calling.
Pray to find peace.
Pray to find a humble aura.

I am thankful for earthly things. Earthly things don't define me. They are meant to bring joy and a humble feeling. To you, my Lord, I pray.

Looks are a God-given gift. We all look the way Jesus says. Some have a unique look. Others are a pretty package. Instead of using them to deceive, to manipulate people into doing things or lying and pretending you have depth, we need to cherish because we age. True beauty and sexiness is in your behavior and how you treat people. They are never forever. They will fade, and all you have left is character. So if you're pretty, people need to remember the time capsule is cruel. So be kind and enjoy the looks while they last. God hates vanity.

I am not gorgeous, but God gave me a tender heart for the world and to be an example of love; to be human first, and a source of love. I am not sexy. I am just me. For me, being sexy is a feeling, which is a result of how you carry yourself with the fellow man. For me, being gorgeous is having a heart and soul, which always puts the human race before his or her own needs. For me, loving what I see in the mirror is far better than fancy words and empty compliments.

It's in the *how*, not *when* you get there. For me, it's about Jesus and His way; the simplicity of prayer and action, one step at a time, always asking God, praying His Father's prayer, seeking His wisdom, knowing, no matter what, He has always provided. He has always come through for me. I have always believed that long before I was intimate with Jesus.

His voice soothes me.
His love saves me.
His Word is the walkway.
He comforts me.
He knows my every need.
He walks beside me.
He gives me strength.
I turn to my alpha, Jesus.

Psalm 10:1-2:
> "The Lord says to my lord sit at my right hand until I make your enemies a foot stool for your feet"

(Point: never fear your doubters nor your naysayers. Hold fast to Jesus).

"The Lord will extend your mighty scepter from Zion; you will rule in the midst of your enemies" (Point: trust God. Ask and receive. Seek and find. Bring to God your cares. Believe in the Father. Don't worry. Be active with God. Love no matter what).

Psalm 89:2:
"I will declare that your love stands firm forever that you establish your faithfulness in heaven itself."

Reflection:
I will always need Jesus, as will you. I will always try to hold His will above my own. I will always turn to God over mere men and the world's ways. You can have eternal life. The flesh is merely a temple for which the spirit is covered for the here and now.

Pray to Jesus everyday, and leave no part of your life untouched.

Psalm 86:1:
"Hear, oh Lord, and answer me for I am poor and needy."

Reflection:
The Lord will provide. He has prosperity lined up. He will replace the needy feeling with sense of fulfillment. He will always delight to hear from you and me. When you ask, you will receive. When you seek, you will find.

Prayer:
Lord, never forsake me. Never leave me behind in the world's battle of struggle. Give me Your ear and grace.

Reflection Recap:
Dream again.
Pray always.
Give God your worries.
Let love in.
Be open to His call.
Share His Word.
Inspire others.
Let love win.
Ask God.
Pray to God.
Don't give up.
Believe in your words.
Speak it to God.
Mean what you say and He will make it happen.
Look to no other, but God Himself.
Be ready to walk with the Majestic One.
Give to Jesus always.
Bring no doubt into life.
Give your best.
Be honest with where you are.

love devotionals.
Love writing;
It's a way to clear your mind.
You can replace the evil one's destruction.
You can have a better mindset.
When you write or read someone else's words, you can relate.
Deep down, we all want to be heard.
Good, bad, and the ugly
You can get a new perspective on an issue you are dealing with.

Closing Prayer:
May my words help.
May my books relax you.
May God let me write devotionals.
May God come alive through my devotionals.

Proverbs 1:2-19

Reflection:
Do not follow others. Do not do what the crowd does because, in the end, it's not the Jesus way. People will deceive you for their own gain and desires. When you let stuff consume you, they rob you; you can't take it with you. When you want something and ask for it, then make sure you are coming from an honest and godly place. Be careful what you wish for and be humble in asking.

Proverbs 1:20-24

Reflection:
We are meant to dream and turn to God. We were meant to rise above the ordinary and live out a destiny from Him. God gives us the way and the truth. If you listen and look, He not only restores them literally, but spiritually, to live better. God doesn't wait for you to decide, nor does He do it all for you. He expects you to be active and do your part. With God, you ask, receive, seek, and find. He wants you to trust Him in life.

Words

They have power;
Strong as weapons and steel.
They have the ability to heal, hurt, and inspire.
Words are the new weapon.
They are used casually, and not much thought goes into them
most of the time.
Yes, we have freedom of speech,
Yet God warns about the power of the tongue.
May you use your words.
May you use them wisely.
Words, communication is always the best way.
So now, let's pray:
Words, may you use them. Words are the voice of God.

Love

Love is the key.
It moves mountains.
We read about it.
We sing about it.
It's the gift that never stops giving.
Love today.
Love tomorrow.
Love everyday.
Don't go a day without love.
God's biggest command says love.
Love thy neighbor as I love you.
He wants you to love.
He wants us all to love.
We need to love.
We are meant to give it away.

Fill your heart.
No matter what, God loves.
When you love, be His love machine.
Love.
Love, and more love.

Life

Live it well.
Never squander it away.
Each new day, God chooses to bring you closer to His destiny for you.
Life.
It's meant to experience the pleasure.
Learn from the pain.
Grow with your faith.
Life.
Never easy or promised that there would be no trials, but God gave you life.
He gave His Son for you.
Life.
Looks at you.
Says, ready or not, I am happening.
So what do you do?
Pray to God.
Be active.
Grow and learn.
Then God says it's your life.

Breathe

When you breathe, you release the pressure of the day.
You invite new life into your soul.
You are to breathe and not hold it in.
Let your stress go.
Breathe.
When you feel the pressure, take a deep breath, in and out,
then say, "God, You are in me."
You are my air supply.
You will give me new life.
Breathe.
It's easy.
It's a stress release.
You do it daily.
Why not be thankful for each new day?
As you breathe, praise God for your life.

Fate

Do we end up where we are supposed to be?
Or do we end up where choices lead us?
We all make choices in life.
The key is not to let them turn into regret.
Maybe the best way is to not repeat the same choices.
Do your best.
I am not totally perfect at doing it myself.
I try to make the best of it.
Life and people get in the way.
Fate.
Not sure about it.
Even I question God on why He does it.

If I shall have a destiny, is it grand in my dreams? Or is it the reality of my day?

Why

Instead of asking why, say to God, "I will listen. I will do my part."
I won't question.
I will, instead, believe there is a reason.
God already knows, so don't worry and get worked up.
But, instead, just do what you can.
Give it an honest attempt.
Pray daily.
Look to Him for an answer.
Take one day at a time;
One step at a time.
Don't run.
Don't try to fast-track.
We have too many whys in our life.
Let's drop some now.
Relax.
Give it to God.
No more whys, just yes to God.

Know

You can know what you want.
You can know what you must do.
Yet you must know to give it to God.
You must know that you have to be active.
God knows what desires are in your heart.
Know.
I now know what my calling is.

Know enough; I can't just give lip service.
I must do what I have to.
Know what my options are.
I will be active and do what I need to.
Knowing is only half the battle.
Prayers, faith, and God; those are the rest.
This must and now know.

I was weak.
I was lost;
Never far from You.
I was scared.
I cried out to You.
You heard me,
Never forsaking me.
You're my Lord.
I love Thee more than myself.
Always wanted.
Trying to be the best me.
I was.
I'm not really sure, but this I know: You give me more, and
for that, You are Lord.
Father.
Forgive me again.
I am only human.
I was weak.
No more.
I was lost, but found Thee.
Never far from You.
Amen.

God

Was a bit shaky.
You gave me a gift.
You gave me Cadie when I needed an ear and a soundboard;
When I needed a friend.
You gave me real human connections.
You love me.
I see that now.
Thank You for my Cadie.
Thank You for my friend;
A voice to communicate;
A set of eyes to see fully and a set of ears to hear Your truth.
Thank You for my life; crazy, but full of promised life.
May You always be the rock of salvation in my heart.

Lord, the world wants to shake me.
Yet You say no.
I choose to say, "Not now, devil."
God has my heart.
His love will give me vision to see and ears to listen.
Both will be my guides.
My mentality,
My physicality,
My emotions,
My spirituality,
My eyes will see,
My ears will listen,
My ambition,
Will all come from You.
I'm not perfect. You know that.
Now I must admit to myself I can do all with You.
I choose to believe.
I choose to be active.

Lord, like the color of my soul, some days are blue and others gray.
Remind me that I must get the right amount of sleep, nutrition, physical activity, and laughter.
These tools are in my arsenal.
You gave me heart and soul.
I may take a few repetitions, but they are my assets.
To health.
To a better way of life; to a calmer and more peaceful existence.
Protect my eyes.
Protect my ears.
Protect my soul.

Mentally Healthy

My thoughts are with God and not always on me.
Physically healthy.
I am getting enough sleep.
I am eating and not worrying about image.
I am taking care of my hearing and emotional health.
Put God first.
Being active on the road and not let the job affect me.
Give it to God.
Spirit.
Read more Scripture.
Read more Bible.
Focus on daily devotion.
Attend Bible study, no matter how tired or stressed.
MPES is my road to God.
Mentally, we must bring our mind one with God.
We must put our thoughts in line with God.
Repeat what we know.

God would say to repeat what He knows and has placed in our hearts.

Mentally.

Means neither giving into nor believing the lies the world places on us.

Mentally, we must say over and over the promises of God.

Know what He says.

What He feels for you and me.

He is not the power, but He is the power to mentally know this.

Emotional

My heart is on my sleeve.

I care too much, yet I know God created me.

I always refer to it as my double-edged sword.

I can feel so much and get hurt.

Emotions are great, and, yet, can be a burden.

I would rather feel than not feel at all; at least I know I am alive.

I may not like the hurt or pain, yet emotions keep me going toward God and His love.

Emotions.

I have many, and feel all of them with the same intensity.

Emotions.

Many songs are written with many feeling emotions.

Physical

Get enough sleep.

I try to get eight hours.

Used to be able to; now, not so much.

So much is on my mind, too much that I get mad at God.

Yet I know I was responsible for it.

You know my free will in all.

Physical.

All about balance.

All four have to be with one.

When you are mentally focused, you are able to stay on track.

Then you get and eat regularly, and you are emotionally at peace.

Finally you get a well-balanced spirit.

Spirit

A lot of things calm it; my two cats, my music, singing, and friends.

Yet when any of other factors of MPES are out of line, then my spirit is not so happy.

Then I must turn to God.

I sometimes yell more than once, and though I do that, He is ready to help.

He may not be direct, but He has a divine way to make me see my faults.

As if He opens the blinders of reality.

Gives me clarity, then a peace comes over me.

A full redemption of MPES.

My Prayer

God, never forsake me.

I know I need You, always.

Even when I'm in a state of walking away, give me grace to come home to You.

No matter my words, I feel my heart and know my true emotions.

Let me see.

Let me hear.

See what I must do.

Hear Your advice.

Physical and in all my MPES.

May the value of my worth be revealed through your love by which all I do is Your will and pray for Your wisdom.

My prayer for MPES.

I look in the mirror today; I see a broken man.

One who has done all right.

I always start with good intentions, which is not always easy.

Has broken the temple and causes ugliness in his self-image.

Has somehow lost his way.

Not just temporary, but way down in the soul.

A fearful man.

One whose emotions are all over the place.

You see a hurting man in need of simplicity.

A longing man in search of love and a way out, but not the kind you think.

A man who cries, yet never loses the hurt.

The man who once wanted to do so much and gave way too much of his heart and soul, only to be beaten down by the game of life.

When I look in the mirror, I see a man who knows Jesus loves him and will never forsake him.

Restore his eyes and ears so he can be what God intended, no matter how many times he wants to give up.

He won't take the easy way out.

Instead, I will seek and dive into the covenant with God.

Accept

I did the damage.

No reversing the damage.

No so-called miracle.

The products may do what they are supposed to if I wasn't
so damaged.
I cannot eat or drink.

Changes

Eat better.
Less sugar.
More sleep.
No daydreaming.
Live in the moment.
Take it one day at a time.
Trust God completely and not half-ass.
Give it to God and be done with the head games.
Listen to God and what He tells you.
Never do I try to give up.
So many times, I have cried.
Not truly given up, though I'd rather cry and have a moment.
Yet I need to remember Rome was not built in a day.
So neither will my mess, which I take full responsibility for.
I will do my part and not let Him do all the work.
I know and must see that.
He only does when you help yourself.
He is not home yet, until then, you must be smart.
Avoid, turn away, and do not get caught up in man's world.

Where did my life go?
It's not where I wanted it to end up.
I was so ready to become someone, somebody, something.
Yet I think I got caught up in the game of comparing.
Trying to embody.
Live up to be just like in the meantime become.
Never satisfied.

Damaged.

Broken.

Hurt my MPES balance, yet with God, I know I can get back, even if I can't change most.

Will have to accept what I can't change and change what I can.

This collection of my thoughts is based on dreaming and not giving up.

It's about hope and prayer, not feeling good about yourself.

Also, finding strength and believing in God's timing.

So I dedicate to the following:
Cadie Hockenbary
My Pastor, Donna Fitchette
My stepmom, Cathy

May this be the first of many books published monthly.
Book One, "Hello, God, It's Me, Can We Talk?"

CPSIA information can be obtained
at www.ICGtesting.com
Printed in the USA
LVHW050420250321
682338LV00019B/1142

9 781662 811555